Azanian Love Song

DON MATTERA

For the children
of our beautiful land,
and to the memory
of our freedom fighters
who gave their lives.

May freedom reign!

The Don Mattera Legacy Foundation

In association with

LAUREN MOOI Publishing

© Don Mattera 2007
© Don Mattera 2024

All rights reserved. No part of this publication may be reproduced, stored or transmitted in any form or by any means, electronic, mechanical, photocopying, recording, scanning, or otherwise without written permission from the publisher. It is illegal to copy this book, post it to a website, or distribute it by any other means without permission.

First published by Skotaville Publishers 1983
Second edition published by Justified Press 1994
Third edition published by The Don Mattera Legacy Foundation 2024
This edition (revised) published by LAUREN MOOI Publishing

ISBN: 978-0-7961-6302-8

Edited by Paul Suiter
Typeset by Gail Day
Cover design by Design Mill
Cover photograph courtesy of The Star
2nd edition printed and bound by O.H. Frewin Printers (Pty) Ltd.
Original copy scanned by ZeroPaper (Pty) Ltd.

Table of Contents

About Don Mattera II
Introduction IV
Previous publications VI

Blood River 1
Day of Thunder 2
Sophiatown 3
I feel a poem 4
The Day they came for our House 5
Submission 7
Fall 8
I saw a man 9
Demented 10
Ashamed 11
Protea 12
Vietnam 13
Friday night 14
On a man hanging 15
Let the children decide 16
Mine workers' song 17
Black plum 18
Man to man 19
At least 20
For a cent 21

The sun has died 22
Cry of Cain 23
Departure 24
Sowing and Reaping 25
Futility 26
Gelvandale 27
Weave 28
Degrees 29
Lament 30
Weekend 31
Quest 32
Strange rhythm 33
Limitation 34
I am not there 35
Blackness Blooms 36
Journey 37
Burning train 38
Offering 39
Fallen fruit 40
Truth 41
And yet 42
After the flowering 43
I watched 44
You would know 45
No time, Black man 46

They think us happy	47
Comparison	48
Expectation	49
Embryo	50
Even I	51
Remember	52
Final hour	53
Child	54
Old woman	59
The poet must die	60
Do you remember	61
Of reason and discovery	62
Tokologo	64
Contamination	66
Mystery	67
I am	68
First victim	69
At the mortuary	70
Heat of our chains	71
If we seek to be free	73
Azanian Love Song	74
No children	75
Curfew	77
A new time	78
I stood	79

Sobukwe 80
I am infinite 81
I sing 82
Dry your eyes 83
Shadows deepen 84
Ordeal 85
Sea and sand 86
Sea of shadows 87
New vision 88
Dying ground 89
Singing fools 90
Deluge 91
Softly 92
Morning 93
Your gift 94
Kumbaya 95
Elegy for Beirut 96
Freedom Fighters 97
Sometimes 98
Giovanni 99
Our sons, our daughters 100
Zimbabwean Love Song 101
Bitter seed 102
Salute the warrior 103
Namibian Love Song 105

A gift of words 106
I am nothing 108
Exiles 110
I will think of you 112
A Song for Mandela 113
We have been here before 115

About Don Mattera

Donato Francisco Mattera has been celebrated as a journalist, editor, writer and poet. He is also acknowledged as one of the foremost activists in the struggle for a democratic South Africa, and helped to found both the Union of Black Journalists and the Congress of South African Writers.

Born in 1935 in Western Native Township (now Westbury) across the road from Sophiatown, Mattera can lay claim to an intriguingly diverse lineage: his paternal grandfather was Italian, and he has Tswana, Khoi-Khoi and Xhosa blood in his veins. Yet diversity was hardly being celebrated at that time; in one of apartheid's most infamous actions, the vibrant multicultural area of Sophiatown was destroyed in 1955 and replaced with the white suburb of Triomf, and the wrenching displacement can be felt in Mattera's writing.

Writing was certainly not an obvious conclusion to his youth, which had been characterized by gangs, violence and jail. Partly under the influence of Father Trevor Huddlestone, Mattera began wielding a pen rather than a knife, yet with equal facility; using the struggle as his subject, he went on to produce a sense of poems, stories and plays of force and originality. The authorities responded by raid-ing his house, imprisoning and torturing him, and banning him for ten years. It was during these tumultuous times that Mattera wrote the poems contained in *Azanian* Love *Song*. These were followed by plays, an autobiography, children's writings and more poetry. All this was accomplished while he worked as a journalist for *The Star*, the *Weekly Mail* (now the Mail & Guardian) and other newspapers.

Mattera is the holder of several prestigious literary awards as well as numerous humanitarian citations, including the Order of lkhamba - Silver (2007), the SA Dept. of Ans & Culture Literary Lifetime Achievement Award (2007), the Crown of

Peace Award (Washington - 2004), the Ambassador of Peace Award (Kenya - 2001), the World Health Organization's Peace Award from the Centre of Violence and Injury Prevention (1997), and the French Human Rights Award for the We Care Trust. He has also been awarded an honorary PhD from the University of Natal.

He continues to serve as an active patron of several well-known charities in Johannesburg.

Introduction

It is some ten years since Don Mattera's *Azanian Love Song* was first published.

I think the time is ripe for an essay in appreciation of this ageless literary activist who makes music with his poetry. To hear his resonant voice speak his poetry is also to wish that he would make tape recordings of his reading. He is a natural poet. 'Natural' because he doesn't strain at a vocabulary of resistance or engage in verbal gymnastics to impress his reader. I mean Don doesn't stretch and tug at words until you seem to hear the poem scream to aching point, about to explode from sheer extravagance of anger, contempt and the diction these emotions program in trashy verse. After ten years, I'm even more impressed by the muted tones in which the poetry comes across. The way a Dizzy Gillespie will play down the sound of his instrument, to modify or avoid the sometimes brash, brassy sound such as that of the big swing bands of the '40s into the '50s, e.g. Count Basie's, without implying that the Count's sound, or still less the Duke's, is inferior.

I seem to be listening to the beat of a funeral song in the poem *The day they came for our house: Sophiatown 1962*. On that memorable wintry day his family haven was bulldozed. 'The sun stood still.' he writes, 'a witness to the impending destruction... The power of destroying / the pain of being destroyed / Dust.' If Freedom's fire is ever quenched, he says, it will be enough to make him shiver, scared that the poet in him will die, his poetry forgotten. For, as he amplifies in another poem, the system wants the poet dead: poets reveal the lies being peddled by those in power. Don's banning was an attempt to kill his poetry. The poet will never see the protea as a flower while 'the soul of [South] Africa struggles to be set free'. For everything we detest and fear under Boer rule has poisoned beauty in the protea for us. A lot of Don's poetry comes over with massive sadness, redeemed though it is by his hope that the black man will rise and march forward to the lion's den.

Heal of our chains is the sole example here of the loud poem whose language flaunts an array of sensational adjectives and overstretched metaphors. Obviously, the poem was activated by the tumultuous and bruising events of 1976, the date of its appearance. For to hurry and instantly respond to such events through the medium of poetry is always likely to fail; especially while the crush and clamour of the event and its spin-offs are vibrating in your very being.

We have here, otherwise, a collection of poems that go directly to the heart. Don falls in the line of poets who created in the momentum of the Black Consciousness decade, its new awareness and self-knowledge. It still finds resonances throughout the '80s and '90s.

The title-poem *Azanian Love Song* is another that is alive with telling images: 'Somewhere in the ghetto a child is weeping... a woman is weeping... a woman writes her legacy on leaves of despair.' How simple and transparent is the statement, yet how moving the rhythm, the pace, how loaded with pain. Not the now-pain of a physical nature. Rather, like the slow grinding pain in an African mother who raises children for a distant future far beyond her grasp.

Don Mattera has known the pain of being banned. 'I know why the caged bird sings' is a line he remembers from an early African American poet, Paul Laurence Dunbar (1872-1906). It was Dunbar in his poem *Sympathy* who created the famous image of a bird that has been banging against the walls of its prison in order to free itself and is bleeding. I salute you, Don Mattera, native son!

Professor Emeritus Es'kia Mphahlele
From: *Tribute,* August 1993

Previous publications

- *Exiles Within* - poetry (The Writers' Forum 1984)
- *Kagiso Sechaba* and *One Time Brother* - two poster plays (Open School 1983)
- *Inside the Heart of love* - poetry (AVS 1997)
- *Memory is the Weapon* - autobiography (published internationally 1987)
- *The Storyteller* - short stories (Justified Press 1991)
- *Five Magil Pebbles* - children's stories (Skotaville 1992)

Azanian Love Song

DON MATTERA

Blood River

Blood River
Is redder than the selling sun in winter
For it relives
The dark lean years
When a pact with God
Was signed and sealed in blood

Small wonder black children weep
On the river banks
When elders are baptized
To the thumping of Ama-Zioni drums
They too recall those lean years
When the settling sun was not redder
Then the River of Blood
Which drowned the black man's liberty

Day of Thunder

Day of thunder
day of blood
in the dusty streets of Sharpeville
thunder roared from Saracen skies
blood flowed from African eyes
when they met the hail of dum-dum.

The calling
the crying
the falling
the dying
of men, women and children
and the cold stern faces of them
who held the thunder
and spat the hail
while my people sang:
  Return Africa,
  Africa return.

  Bitter was that day

Sophiatown

Once teeming byways
Now emit an unearthly odour
    strange,
        unfamiliar
        to my senses

This Christmas day
Has lost the fervour of olden times
Buildings lie beaten by bulldozers
And scavengers' rake
The skeletal dreams
Of a dispossessed people

Guns that drove us from our nests
Stain our feathers with Sharpeville blood
On that unforgotten hour
When Herod's men trampled the dark folk
Who sang freedom songs

The steeple clock
Records the seizure of our dreams:
Why
do we lie
in the dust
Like clowns
in a receding twilight
Laughing at the dying clay

I feel a poem

Thumping deep, deep
I feel a poem inside
wriggling within the membrane
of my soul;
    tiny fists beating,
    beating against my being
    trying to break the navel cord,
        crying, crying out
        to be born on paper

    Thumping
    deep, so deeply
    I feel a poem,
        inside

The Day they came for our House
Sophiatown, 1962

The sun stood still
in the sullen wintry sky
a witness
to the impending destruction.

Armed with bulldozers
they came
to do a job
nothing more
just hired killers.

We gave way
there was nothing we could do
although the bitterness stung in us,
in the place we knew to be part of us
and in the earth around we stood.
Slow painfully slow
clumsy crushers crawled
over the firm pillars
into the rooms that held us
and the roof that covered our heads,

We stood.
Dust clouded our vision
We held back our tears
It was over in minutes.

Done.

Bulldozers have power.
They can take apart in a few minutes
all that had been built up over the years
and raised over generations
and generations of children.

The power of destroying
the pain of being destroyed,

Dust …

Submission

With earnest face
And watchful eye
I know the disgrace
Of seeing men die

I have seen a nation grope
In dark despair
Searching for hope
That wasn't there

Dim burns Freedom's flame
As violent men conspire
To quench its name
And place on the sacrificial pyre
Those who oppose their diabolical desire

Here,
Beneath
nature's
sky
A poet shivers
Afraid to die

Fall

Many
things
fall
in a slum

For
it
is
a place of
falling …

Even the people's anguished cries
Rise to fall against skies

A woman falls in the shadows
And is possessed
The money will feed a hungry child

A man falls by his brother's hand
His blood forms a crimson necklace
On the semi-tarred road

A dog falls
To lick the township's wounds
Was Lazarus not better off?

I saw a man

I saw a man
> I saw a woman
> holding hands
> on a lonely road
> at a lonely hour,
> and I thought about you

Tell me, Beloved
> why there are lonely people
> and I will show you tears in the sea

Demented

Demented
Restless
Searching for answers
Making equations
Needing peace,
I walked
Out of Slumville
To the hurst
Where the white folk live
There rose the big city
A monolithic monster
Burning with neon flame
Against a hollow in the sky
I bent and kissed the soil
A current rent my being
O land of my people
Earth
Salt
Blood of my kinsmen
Fill me with love

Demented
Still needing peace
I returned
And Slumville waited

Ashamed

The eye of God
Looks down ashamedly
On the council shacks
That stand like men condemned
Before a firing squad

The search of dead animals
Urine and human dung
Give the township its body odour

Dirty rags and debris
Provide floral decorations
In this garden of hopelessness

In the shacks or streets
Near some broken wall or tree
Wasted men and women love their slum
As they would sexual pleasure
It is one condition of being coloured
In Western Township,
  Living without honour
  Dying with shame

Protea

The Protea
Is not a flower
It is a dome of fluttering white flags,
Tombs of Afrikaner relics
And monuments of ox-wagons
Dipped in blood

It is the flight of the Black spear
Flung in hostile fear
Of lost possession
Conquered manhood,
Broken pride

It is the tears
Of my bonded brothers and sisters
Falling on Pretoria's marble steps
The voiceless victims of subjugation

And so the Protea
Can never ever be a flower
Not while the Soul of South Africa
Struggles to be set free

Vietnam

I see hands
holding death
bullets fleeting
through jungle mesh
to a dreaded meeting
with human flesh

Cracking of bone
ripping of lung
agony on a dying man's tongue
I fail to comprehend
why men are called
to such a wasted end

Vietnam, Vietnam
land of fertility
dipped in blood

Friday night

Night rolls quietly
no sounds stir the heavy air
for a while all is still as death

Two shadows waiting
a female third is out baiting
the unwary sober or drunk

Their youthful bodies soaked in moonbeams
but moonbeams are not prettier
than a dying body soaked in blood

Two shadows flashing knives
wasting lives.
They know,
we know,
God knows
Friday night is rolling death

On a man hanging

Who hears
The wild wind banging
In objection to a man hanging

Who hears
The chains clanging
When the limp body is dangling
To appease society's vindictive clamouring

Can the debt be paid with hanging
Will there be no end
To such wild banging
I see strange fruit
In the hangman's orchard

Let the children decide

Let us halt this quibbling
Or reform and racial preservation
Saying who belongs to which nation
And let the children decide
It is their world

Let us burn our uniforms
Of old scars and grievances
And call back our spent dreams
and the relics or crass tradition
That hang on our malignant hearts
And let the children decide
For it is their world

Mine workers' song

Egoli
>Beyond the yellow dunes
>turning, spinning, laughing wheels
>faster train
>devour the track
>there can be no turning back

>City of cites
>Built on the crushed visions of our fathers
>christened by the salt of mothers mourning
>their prodigals

Egoli
>Lights of sorcery and passion
>the last ride
>the last ride
>slipping on wheels
>laughing on tracks
>>I'm coming
>>I'm coming

Black plum

This land
This soil so stiff-necked and proud,
This beautiful earth is a garden
And I am the fruit
Squeezed of energy
Drained of love
Dried of hope

A garden watered by anguish,
fertilized by the tears
of my people,
strewn with the seeds
of their lives

I am the black plum
Fruit of Mama Africa
Spirit that cries out beyond the horizon
The soul seeking emancipation

I am Africa

Man to man

Great God
      I sometimes wonder how strong you are
      what awful cosmic tension
      throbs inside your restless brain
      why in the scheme of conception
      did you include pain

      If we could meet on even terms
      man to man
      you stripped of power
      I of fear,
      I'd lift my shirt and show you scars
      wide as the moon, black as the stars

      If only you could meet
      in the ghetto or the street
      you stripped of the power of death
      I of its fear,
      I'd go away from you
      and you would cry to have me back
      perhaps I shall return to wipe your eyes
      for we could not have a God that cries

At least
On the birth of my son, Malcolm

This day at least
Let me see the hours through
Without a wince of discontent
As I drop the heavy cloak
Of bitter resolve
To welcome the infiltration
Of warmth
And life
And love
And beauty

This day at least
Let me be moved away
From the ghosts of pained exhortation
That lacerate the heart, embittered emotion

For these brief
Somewhat fleeting hours
While the crisp laughter
Of newly-born winds fills me deeply,
O my land
O my country

At least for this untroubled day
Let me unclench my hands
To stroke the yellow flowers
That smiled when my son
Cried himself into life.

At least …

For a cent

Each morning
Corner of Pritchard and Joubert,
Leaning on a greasy crutch
Near a pavement dustbin
An old man begs
Not expecting much.

His spectacles are cracked and dirty
He does not see my black hand
Drop a warm cent into his scurvy palm
But instinctively he mutters:
      Thank you my Baas!

Strange
      That for a cent
      A man can call his brother Baas

The sun has died
For Malcolm

Wounded and bleeding
the sun closed its eye
and sinking slowly
it began to die

Trees noticed the sad spectacle
lowered their heads
as tears of leaf fell
from the cheeks of their boughs

Above birds in solemn flight
formed a guard of honour
for the dying monarch

A lark sounded the last post
and the flag of night was lowered
as the world covered itself
in a black cloak of mourning

A star showed the resting-place
and crickets chirped in sad repine:
the sun has died!
the sun has died!
the sun has died!

But the sun will rise again
and with it
the dreams of children
and the hopes of men
and women…

Cry of Cain

The cry of Cain
is heard again
cry of suffering
jab of pain
how it echoes ever deeper
Am I my brother's keeper

Must I fret or care
when he calls a god
who is not there

Go my brothers
and wash your hands
in the pool of indifference
but mind your silver crosses
might pull you down
and it would be sad
to see the self-righteous drown

Departure

I grow tired
and want to leave this city
seething in unrest and injustice
I am leaving

No,
I have already left
Look for me
on the banks of the Nile
or under some spreading tree

I shall be sleeping
the sleep of freedom
don't wake me
leave me to dream
my dream of departure
from a city
seething in unrest,
void of pity

I grow weary of eating brine
and I hunger for desert fruit

Sowing and Reaping

See my dark brothers sowing seed
Which in time will be growing
High on the master's field
Abundantly the yield
Increases in his barns and nests
Food aplenty for the verminous pests

Yet what of us who sow
And of them who reap
What of the harvest can we show
But the meagreness of our keep

Even in our bruised bowing
Of toil and ploughing
We find a moment to sing of the sunset
And the dawn when we will claim our debt

Futility

The workday ends
To crowded trains
That smell of sweat and disinfectant.
The walk through the township
Alerts the senses in precaution
Against the threat of cold steel.
The eager smiles of children
And the soft caress of a loving wife
Fails to soothe the troubled heart.
Sleep eludes the eyes
And fear of facing another barren day
Gnaws like a cancer in the belly.
The rise from bed
The stroll in the cool night air
In search of peace of mind
Then a loud banging at the door
Tells of a knifed body
Covered with newspaper
A few yards from the house

Gelvandale

*After the shooting of protesters who
campaigned against bus fare incenses*

My spirit moved among you
in that open square
when your cries for justice
were answered by bullets
that ripped your flesh
cut your veins
broke your bones

I was the child sleeping
in that mother's womb
awakened by the fire
of sizzling steel
mine the blood
that dyed the Gelvandale dust
yours the passage
through which it flowed

I know you're sad
it is the same with me
but we must not let them bruise us down
they must not bruise us down

Weave

Listen,
If I could weave
thread upon thread upon thread,
I would bring you a cloak
made of all the Seasons:

Summer
To crown you with Song

Winter
To expose your spirit to Love

Autumn
To blow away your leaves of Pain

Spring
To adorn you with the Promise
Of better days

Degrees

There is no hurt
Quite like being unloved
No peace for the lonely heart
Save death

Will the tumour in my fevered mind
Ever cease its violent throbbing
Will laughter ever flow from the vein of my pen

There is no hurt
Quite like being unloved,
Unwanted
Among one's own
In one's own land

Lament

I weep for you my country
That you must some day bear testimony
To the final folly
When men turn against each other

When those who kill for seeming love
Die for lack of it
When the trodden rise up in anger

I weep for you South Africa
And dread the long nightfall
We so hastily call

I weep for you my country
For was it not you that suffered us to birth
Your sustaining breasts
That nourished our tender limbs
As we sucked from a common vein
And pride was heavy on your heart

But how is it now
Sweet mother of my life and love
That our white brothers
Gather crops from fields
They have not ploughed
While we the dark sons
Feed on bitter fruit

Weekend

Four days to crowded platforms
with eyelids dressed
in curtains of unfinished slumber,
they wait for their train

Payday marks a pause in toil
and bottle stores burst with profit
a weekend is in the making

Drunken bodies everywhere,
behind shebeens in muddy alleys
silhouetted against shacks of rusty tin,
ravaged,
        wrecked
                in webs of sin

Women singing
ribald and inviting
men buying
choosing or fighting
and wax candles flickering
the terror of a weekend dying

Quest

I am the quest
Beginning without end
My spirit moved
The chanting tribes,
I am no stranger
To this earth

It is mine

Each stone has felt my stride
Sand grains tremble at the inquisition
Of my being,
Hills pillow my thoughts
All mountains know me

I am Kilimanjaro

I have lived in every stream
Walked in the dark waters
Where ancestors were worshipped and feared
I wept when rivers were wanting,
The seas were salted by my tears
I am the Limpopo
Giver of life
Alpha without omega
I am the quest,
I am Afrika

Strange rhythm

There is magic
In your chanting
In the goatskin drum
You beat in prayer

I listen
And a strange rhythm
Pulsates in me
In my soul
In my mind
The sound of Ama-Zioni
Stripping me naked
Revealing my sin
As I sink into the river
To meet forgotten kin

Limitation

When I asked for bread
They gave me the wheatfield
And told me they loved me

When I asked for water
They gave me the well
And told me they cared

Because I believed they loved me
Because I believed they cared
I asked them for my freedom

But they took back the wheatfield
And took back the well
Tightened the chains
And told me I asked too much

I am not there

When I told them of my love
They laughed and turned their backs

When I told them of my need
They scoffed and counted their treasure

When I told them of my anger
They threatened me with guns and banishment

Now they hear that I hate them
And they turn around to love me
But I'm not there

Blackness Blooms

Night drops liquid darkness
From a wound in the sky
Men look on my blackness
As a weed that must die

Here in the dark
I feed on bitter bark
And my hands bleed
From planting thorny seed

Come morning
Come glorious light
Return justice
Heal my broken sight

Ah, black sunbeams fall on the slope
Bringing new light to fulfil my hope
Ever conscious of their sacred duty
Then sweet, sweetly my blackness blooms
And becomes my beauty

Journey

Sometimes
    the soul
    will soar
    in flight
    above the dark veil
    of night
    and like an eagle
    hover above the quiet plane
    searching for a place
    to shed its pain

Burning train

Train, train
Burning train,
Tortuous pain
The bitter past lives again

People entangled in the fiery mesh
Piteous spectacle of falling flesh
Screaming terror
Of the last breath
Sickening horror
Of a burning death

Of what avail are tears
So scant of relief
To such immeasurable grief
And gripping fears

I hear a woman calling her child
who stands lame
Overcome by the devouring flame
Which dances menacingly wild

Others cursed while others cried
Some wished they had rather died
Profound was their anguish
Moving, their morbid wish

Brothers white, brothers black
Remove charred bodies off the track
Driven by single human compassion
For those who died in so brutal a fashion

Offering

To say
That you love
And offer it
To a dream

To say
You love that dream
And offer it to man

To say
You love man
Yet offer him to God
As Cain did his brother

To say rather no such love
Nor dream
Nor offering
        and what of no God?

Fallen fruit
For Hawa Timol… *on the death of her son Ahmed
who fell from the 10th floor at John Vorster Square*

Weep mother Hawa
For the fruit of your womb
Fallen from a tree of stone

Weep for the earth
That caught his blood
And for them who dig his grave

Weep for his people
And for his land
Weep for yourself

But more than all,
Weep for the shattered fragment called justice
Crushed beneath the jackboot

Truth

Truth
        Like broken glass
        lies scattered
        on the highway of life

        But in the quiet hour
        when the streets are resting
        a solitary figure crouches
        to gather the pieces

        And justice
        looks on from a distance
        unmasked,
                unmoved,
                        unclean

And yet

I have known silences
    Long and deep as death
    When the mind questioned the logic
    Of my frailty
    In the imminence of my destruction
    By men ruled, ravaged by power lust

I have known deep silences
    When thoughts like angry waves
    Beat against the shores of my mind
    Revealing scares of brutal memories
    And the murder of my manhood

    And yet,
    I cannot hate
    Try as I want,
    I cannot hate.

    Why?

After the flowering

How sweetly the boy laughed
Each morning
As the bus sped to town

I loved the sound,
In him I spied
Some forgotten phase of my childhood

Then they told me he was dead
And something passed out of me
Like a spring retiring
After the flowering

Laughter still rings,
But cannot sustain
Or fill the vacuum
Of a retired spring
When a little boy laughed

I watched

I watched
The sun weep
In its sinking
Once-proud rays covered
By a cloak of dark
A flame reduced
To a dying spark

You would know

If you could enter my body
And your deft fingers
Rummage the webs of my mind,
You would know my love
Day does not pass into eager night
Without your name burning itself into my soul,
Into every ventricle and fibre of my being

Night and day, day and night
It is the same
One does not become the other
Without me calling your name
If only you could enter
You would know my love

No time, Black man

Stand, Black man,
Put that cap back
On your beaten head

Look him in the eye
Cold and blue
Like the devil's fire
Tell him enough,
Three centuries is more
Then you will take,
      Enough
Let him hear it
If he turns his face and sneers
Spit and tell him shit
It's all or nothing,
He's got all
And you have nothing

Don't bargain with oppression
There's no time, man,
Just no more time
For the Black man
To fool around

They think us happy
Thoughts of a mine dancer

They think us happy
because we hide our anguish in song
stamp our shackled feet
until red drips from the cracks

They smile
and we smile,
we only smile
because they smile
and they think us happy

Let us remove our masks
of artificial merriment
reveal the wrinkles
of our quiet anger
wash the clay from our bodies
and let them see the scars

Perhaps they know, perhaps not
but dammit they must be told
we have had enough!

Comparison

Trees do not fret
When winter's sharp breath
Kisses their boughs
Robs them of beauty
Leaving them naked and exposed

The trees know spring will return
Like a longing lover
To caress their limbs with new life
And adorn their breasts
With flowers and fruit

But what of the Black child
Stripped by centuries
Of oppressive winters

Is she not fairer than all earth's trees
More precious than flowers or fruit
That she merits the delay
Of a faltering spring
Which promised freedom
To her mother and her people.

    O that spring should hurry
    And crown her with liberty
    That it should come now, now

Expectation

Many sunsets
Gold and crimson
Have dripped on the horizon,
Weeping for the dying day

Many dawns
Have risen
In timely resurrection
From their cradles of light

Sunsets and dawns
Dawns and sunsets
I have seen them all
But when,
O when will I see that day
When love will walk the common way
To heal my wounded people
And break the shackles around their hearts

Embryo

Now Night winces
In labouring pain
To give birth
To a new day

My eyes are heavy and deep
And will not succumb
To the soft caress of sleep
They wait the pregnant Night
To release its child of light

Now Night smiles in relief
Her pain is gone
I hear the first birth-cry
Of a new dawn

If only,
God
If only out of the womb of turmoil
Peace would be born
And out of hatred, love
If only
God ...
If only

Even I

Only through Nature's decree
Does the buzzing brown bee
Rest its weary wings on the sweetpea
Even I am given that wonder to see

Only Nature's heart-strings
Quiver, when the silent rain sings
Of the joy true love brings
Even I can hear such sweet things

Only she weeps for the vain deed
Of man in his selfish need
As he reaps fruit of arrogant seed
From a bitter harvest toiled with greed

Only her bosom bears the strain
When the parched earth cries for rain
From a warped and bloodless vein
And she chooses me to share her pain

But only Man continues blind
Stumbling in vain to find
The path of lasting peace of mind
And Nature in compassion, shields from behind
Only man continues blind

Remember

Remember to call at my grave
When freedom finally
Walks the land
That I may rise
To tread familiar paths
To see broken chains
Fallen prejudice
Forgotten injury
Pardoned pains

And when my eyes have filled their sight
Do not run away for fright
If I crumble to dust again
It will only be the bliss
Of a long-awaited dream
That bids me rest
When freedom finally walks the land

Final hour

When horizons weep bloody tears
You may reach out, white brother
For the fruit of compassion
But your hand will return empty
Like the desolate orchard of your heart.

Yet even at that final hour
my bleeding limbs may land
To lift your cringing frame
Against the bitterness of my pain
Perhaps you may come to love me then,
Though it may be too late
And I will weep for both of us
As we drown
      drown
      drown

Child
For my daughter Noëleen

The leaves of my tree
grow brown and thin
soon they will fall to earth
and be forgotten

Much fruit has withered
only a few strong boughs remain
but they too will be broken
by the fury that will sweep our land

But of all my fruit
of all things dear and close to my heart,
are you and the hope that is manifest
in your being
you, the offspring of an invincible dream

All my seeking, my fervent cries
and the death of longing are but distant echoes
my wounds mere relics
yet all I ask of you
is that you should remember me
for what I tried to do, tried to offer
so that a new bright sun would rise on your day;
that a portion of my dream for the freedom of my people
would find a place in your song,
my name and those who marched with me
be recorded on your scroll

What does a man live for
if not to be remembered by his beloved

I wanted to offer you sonnets
and poems of springbuds unfurling to the sunlight
sing about the fir trees pointing at God
but how can I sing of the tree
when beneath it my brothers lie bleeding
and their wounds unfurl the horror of existence
and their prayers are cries of death
and their hearts curse God

Yet amid all the hate and hostility
I do not hate those who hold us in servitude
through I have tried hard to do so,
I just cannot hate

Perhaps it is a weakness on my part
perhaps the folly of the oppressed
is that we do not hate enough
or that we love too much
but it is a truism that revolutions
are born out of love;
love for land and liberty
love of humanity and love of oneself

I have watched many suns sink
seen phantom shadows raise their ominous banners
and I have heard my name called
while dreams, desires of a lifetime
were whittled under violent feet

I hold the bloody scroll
with shaky, awe-struck hands
the cup will not pass untouched
by the lips that hunger after justice

How often have I asked God
whether there was something we missed
or a teaching that went unheeded
from the prophets in whose shadows we walked

But you blood is changing;
a vibrant light glows in your eyes
a sacred fire of unseen power within you
claims its bounty of life
tomorrow belongs to you
yours through the strength and defiance
that flows in the struggle carved from God's image

The world is teeming with unrest
everywhere men are fighting to be heard
to walk upright in the land of their fathers
it is no different in our continent
nor in our country where the tin gods
teach their offspring to despise and humiliate us

Greed, selfishness and hypocrisy
have blinded most white people
verily, they live by the sword

Yet there are many good, well-meaning
justice-loving white folk
men and women of conscience
who sacrifice their days that others might be free

Those who did not conform were broken
those who refused to break
were imprisoned or killed
others persecuted to self-exile

but many millions remain silent
enjoying the ill-gotten harvest

I am not influencing you to hate whites
I could not ask such a thing
for it would negate my own humanity
the enmity I feel is for the denial for the black dignity
for the sacred right to love unhindered

I tell you that even finer emotions,
those which sustain us with inner succour
when debasement exacts its toll on our lives,
are now the white man's pastime
and God is made the lie with which we are deceived

But as there are evil white people
so are there black ones
who have become the tools
with which we are fooled and indoctrinated
black men and women who crawl
for the colonial crumbs of comfort
selling their souls for money

Child, I look at the slow decaying
of our people in the cities
in the dry foodless reserves
in the prisons, and a thousand angry rivers
rush inside of me:
the deaths they die will not be in vain,
they are the foundation of your freedom

I look at you and the fear I had for death falters
as I touch your dimpled hands
drink of your warm laughter

certain that you would outlive the tempest
which must first lash the land
in order to set it free

Yet it was in a dream
and it was by the river
that I heard the plaintive voices of men in chains
black men naked and shining singing the slave's song:
How long; Lord, how long?
and the moon fell on the shimmering water
lighting up their faces and I was among them
shackled but singing

So that our voices rose heavy with sound
breaking the fetters that held us bondage

And children came with seed
and where we stood,
they planted a new people

These words I give you
as a testament of my deepest love for you
and for our beloved land
written in the hope that you will remember
those valiant folk who marched with me
and in the remembering, cherish the legacy
bequeathed to you through their blood
in the final hope that a new bright sun
will rise on your tomorrow …

Old woman
From a photograph of Diana Green, aged 96

Time's pins have pierced my limbs
Rivers of wrinkle
Bend and twist on my aged face
Eyes have lost their sparkle

I am old now

It was not always so
Once Time and I were partners
We chased the setting sun
Through fields of sunflower and corn
And there was fire in my eyes
Yellow and orange like my skin

And I was young

Those were the days
Before machines gave birth
To concreate cities
When you could buy a pound
For two pennies
See a rainbow smile
And catch a bowl of sunbeams
Dripping on the horizon

But those days are gone
And now I am old

The poet must die
*For James Matthews and Gladys Thomas
after their poems were executed*

The poet must die
her murmuring threatens their survival
her breath could start the revolution;
she must be destroyed

Ban her
Send her to the Island
Call the firing-squad
But remember to wipe her blood
From the wall,
Then destroy the wall
Crush the house
Kill the neighbours

If their lies are to survive
The poet must die

Do you remember

It is a deep and sacred experience
    to love
    and be loved by you.
The vision of our first consummation
    Immortalised by your purity
    Still fills and sustains
    The fibres of my being
And yet again last night
    I saw your face
    In the palms of my hands
    Burning with a fire
    Foreign to my soul.
And I wept
    Not for the pain
    Nor for the ecstasy
    But for the gift of love
    And the unity of our spirits
    On that fateful day,
    When soft, sweet pain
    Lulled you to sleep in my arms

    Do you remember?

Of reason and discovery
After the killings of black miners at the
Carletonville Mine in the Transvaal

I have dispensed with reasoning
It blinded me to many wrongs
Nearly robbed me of sanity
Once I reasoned with the whiteman's evil,
Saw his crimes against my people
As weakness and human folly
      God would right the wrong, they said
But nobody said when
I have dispensed with reasoning
It clouds a blackman's vision
Blunts his wrath, makes him tolerant of oppression
      I have discovered, yes
The reason for all this hurt
This long deep searching of scanning the godless sky
For the suspended reply
I have discovered, yes
The fault not in the god nor in the pain
But in the sufferer
Who makes virtue of his anguish
Waiting meekly on the god for deliverance
Though white scavengers rip life
From battered black bones

        I have discovered, yes
The yoke is comfortable
When the belly is full
And there is time to pray for peace
While police guns rattle on mine dunes
In the name of white survival
        I have discovered, yes
That an ounce of gold
Exceeds the value
Of a blackman's life
And that there is no more time
To reason and to pray
        I have discovered, yes

Tokologo

Now when dirges
burst the monotony of our lives
when black hearts seek solace
in values foreign and false
and forsake the sanctity of old customs,
now, would I die for a new anthem
a deep and sonorous march
plaintive yet plundering
angry yet committed
protesting yet personifying
our black cries

A singing tree
telling the turmoil of our time
our beginning
our destiny,
singing it in rich song
O sing, Afrika,
sing me a Freedom song
chant in the glow of sunset
in jungle frames
around the sacrifice
and yellow flames

Sing it, Mother in the ghetto
where laughter masks the black man's pain
where men move on bended knees
raped by colonial terror
Sing it in the prison cells
and tombs and dungeons
where martyrs lie thirsting
for the new sunrise
Sing me a song of Freedom
that I may rise
from the quagmire of debasement
and take my rightful place
among free men

Contamination
For the banned and the house-arrested

Only from the corner of your eye
Must you look to see
If I am looking
To see you look away

Do you recall those midnight knocks
You made at my door
When you spoke of fear and concern
Do you remember how you cried on my shoulders
Sharing the silent innermost pains
And do you remember
How your children clamoured around
And you told them to someday be like me
How proud I was when I lifted to kiss them
Nearly smothering their souls

But now you look away
For fear of contamination
Who can tell what the morrow brings
For the leper who walks alone

Mystery

It is a mystery
why we go on at all
when the odds stand against us
so tenaciously

We shall never know
not for all the telling
and the tears
and the faded hope we cling to
nor for the muffled voices
that urge us on from the darkness

It is a mystery that we still walk
these thorny roads of commitment
while gunshots crack the night air
and near us flow the pools of death

I am

I am
      a tree
            standing
                    in the breath
                    of an eternal autumn
                    stripped and naked
                    my spirit calls out:
                    clothe me, Lord
                    cover me
                    with one thread
                    of Sacred Fabric
                    that love may blossom
                    from my soul

                    clothe me, Lord
                    clothe me

First victim

A bullet burnt
Into soft dark flesh

A child fell

Liquid life
Rushed hot
To stain the earth

He was the first victim

And now
Let grieving willows
Mark the spot
Let nature raise a monument
Of flowers and trees
Lest we forget the foul and wicked deed

At the mortuary
After a visit to the government mortuary

there is no sea
in the golden city
the salt you taste
flows from the eyes of black women
weeping for their sons and daughters
who fell for a lullaby:
sweet and low, sweet and low
deathwind blow, blow
June is ablaze with bodies that glow
where will the black fireflies go
ask Jesus he might know

Heat of our chains

What dreams and visions we clutched
In our frantic search for life
Are singed by the heat of our chains
    Nothing remains
    But anger,
    At ourselves, at God
    Reconciliation and amity
    Drown in a whirlpool of unrelenting dogma
    What hope existed for a bloodless revolt
    Now lies shattered
    in a million fragments of despair
    There can never be asylum for expediency
    There is no bloodless war
    We scanned the sky
    For something new and clean
    All we found was enmity
    Pumping our fragile veins
    With new excitement
    Filling our bodies with song:
    Life is a flower
    in a white garden
    of doom
    Though they steal our petals
    They keep the plant
    In bloom

O Freedom
>Though we have not touched
>Your ebony face nor slept beside you
>Yet would we rise up in your name
>To meet and fight the terror
>That darkens our streets.
>No more the sacrifice of our children
>No more the shouts of frightened hearts
>What the soldiers have taken from us
>We shall reclaim
>What bitterness
>Haunts our agony
>Will crown our victory
>Enrich our joy
>And if we must weep
>Let us weep gently,
>Committing our pain
>To our cause
>And with one blow
>Silence these fiends
>Who laugh as we die

If we seek to be free

If we seek to be free
yet fear to die,
Let us at least honour those who serve
And ask not why

Azanian Love Song

Like a tall oak
    I lift my arms to catch the wind
    with bruised fingers
    and somewhere in the ghetto
    a child is born;
    a mother's anxiety and pain
    hide in a forest of hope.

Like a straight pine
    I point my finger at God
    counting a million scars
    on my dreams
    and somewhere in the ghetto
    a child is weeping
    a woman writes her legacy
    on leaves of despair.

Like a weeping willow
    I drop my soul
    into a pool of fire
    somewhere in a dark sanctuary
    I hear the sound of a freedom song:

    The child has risen
    and walks defiantly
    towards the lion's lair
    undaunted,
    unafraid

No children

There are no children
Hippos, guns still stalk
The silent streets;
Blood, pain
Nature an uncaring anger

No children in Soweto, Langa, Mannenberg,
Not a child left in Sharpeville
Dead
Jailed
Crippled
Blinded
Tortured, yes
The children have all become adults

And so, let no-one lament
Those unlived, lost summers
Nor weep for the shadows
That once were children
Laughing in the sand

Let us not walk too gently
When we pass their graves
Out footsteps must stir their sleep
The dead must learn to talk
The living learn to die

Jesus hymns fill the townships:
'Fast falls the eventide'
And queues of mourning mothers
Search for slain children
'When other helpers fail ...'
But death can lift a man
It can reshape a trembling people
And replenish it with purpose,
Give it new life

Let no black man weep
Let no white man weep
There is purpose in death

Curfew

And after all the bloodletting
There was a deep silence
In the land
The bloodletters
Called it peace
And a triumph
For law and order
But beyond the ravaged ghetto
Sirens ring an encouraging curfew
To a frightened white electorate:
The children
Have all been driven
Off the streets
Peace has been restored

Amen

A new time

Beyond the ash-heaps of broken days
The tortured cries of starving folk
Drown in a flood of young voices
Swelling thick with the promise
Of a new time

Children singing from the graves
It is their year
All years belong to the children
The beginning years
And the end years
Earned with their blood

I stood
For Nyoka

I stood in the shadow
Of your quiet thoughts
And saw
Particles of broken dreams and
Silenced,
Muffled,
Emotions

I saw and knew
As if I always had known
That like me,
Many a spring had fled your life
Somewhere in the narrow straits of time
We traversed a common path of pain
And waited for love
In vain

For a fleeting moment
I glimpsed on your childhood
And saw
Your laughing eyes in the warm sun
And the tall, tall grass bent
To cover our nakedness

In the quiet shadows
Of your thoughts
I saw my seasons fade

Why?

Sobukwe
On his death

It was our suffering
and our tears
that nourished and kept him alive
their law that killed him

Let no dirges be sung
no shrines be raised
to burden his memory
sages such as he
need no tombstones
to speak their fame

Lay him down on a high mountain
that he may look
on the land he loved
the nation for which he died

Men feared the fire of his soul

I am infinite

I am
Infinite
Indestructible
Did not
My dark veins
Nourish
The hungry earth
Tears quench
The thirst
Of rivers

I am
The tortured
Unavenged
Lover
Unloved
Dying
For a burial ground
To tell
The hour of my deliverance

I am Africa
Infinite
Indestructible

I sing

I sing my dirge at daybreak,
watch the ghosts of despair
Blot out the sun's eyes
And flesh that mirrors truth, dies

I reach out
Across the sleeping years
To awaken the tomorrow
Of my beginnings:
Dead days emerge
To shed their rags
And ancient, muffled dreams
Speak anew, afresh
The language of love
I spoke in innocence

Streets are alive once more
And a symphony of unbroken songs
Cascades on the tranquil sea
Of my mother's warm after-birth
Which gave me claim to life

But now shadows
Fall on my soul to seal my lips
And bursts of blood in the dusty townships
Rupture the twilight dream
Suspended between today and tomorrow

Nothingness is my inheritance,
I am
A stranger
In my own land

Dry your eyes
On the death of Sebastian,
my sister's 10-month-old son

Dry your eyes my sister
though the child you carried
in your childhood is dead
your breasts will regain their roundness
and your body blossom
like this spring day
ready to bear new fruit

Dry your eyes my little one
sadness does not become so young a face
neither does motherhood

Shadows deepen

Shadows deepen
      and sunlight pours its parting rays
      in a quiet corner
      of my heart

Sounds of longing
      beat like a drum
      in every ventricle
      of my body

I saw your face again
      in the petals
      of drooping flowers
      and in my daughter's face

In the night, like some nocturnal orphan
      I called your name
      hoping you would come to me
      in my dreams

Ordeal

Death-winds refuse to be gagged
And for me
The old ordeals will be relived
Eyes must once more embrace
The woe of my unfreeness

And so
I traverse the dark streets
A nocturnal dreamer
Seeking some deeper meaning from life
Across these barricades
Touching hearts as feeble as mine
Searching for strength to carry on

Sea and sand

Sea and sand
My love
My land,
      God bless Africa
Sea and sand
My love
My land
      God bless Africa
But more the South of Africa
Where we live
Bless the angry mountains
And the smiling hills
Where the cool water spills
To heal the earth's brow

Bless the children of South Africa
The white children
And the black children
But more the black children
Who lost the sea and the sand
That they may not lose love
For the white children
Whose fathers raped the land

Sea and sand
My love, my land
God Bless Africa

Sea of shadows

In this dark sea of shadows
where black dreams die still-born
we shred the veil of hell
seeking the warmth
of love's hidden fire

But the cinders
of burnt days
scatter in the wind,
blown by passion
soured by pain

In this dark sea of shadows
why do we cry our cause
to an unheeding tribe
who mock our grief
and plot the destruction of our house

New vision
For Ephraim Nkondo

Look
At me,
I am the Future
    Time ebbs out
    Like water sucked
    By ruthless seasons
    And Yesterday shrivels
    Unfulfilled,
    Empty

    Today hobbles
    Passively
    Like a Gandhi
    Bathing in the sleeping Ganges

    Yes, look at me
    I am Tomorrow!

    My eyes are the windows
    Of a new hope
    A new vision

    My ears are drums
    Beating the heritage
    Of my native land
    My face, the banner of Promise
    Look at me,
    I am Tomorrow, manifest

Dying ground

The elephants came
And brought with them a crookery
of God and compassion,
Took the verdant land
With psalms and gunpowder
And proclaimed a covenant in his name.
Today,
The fetters bite deeper
Cruelty is resolute,
Genocide defined.

Lo, beyond our motherland
Black children eat their future
From bloodied pots
Where freedom is sown
With the seeds of valiant struggle.

The harvest is bitter for the settlers
And now the last exodus gathers frenzy
The trail points southward
To the last outpost
(A haven to their whiteness)
Sensing the final hour
They hurry to the sacred sand
(Our conquered land)
But let them come
O let the white elephants draw near.

What would be their refuge
Will yet become
Their dying ground.

Singing fools

This mockery of fondest love
And exhibitions of peace
Behind private dinner halls
Must be crushed for the lie
They perpetuate at the altar of uhuru

For there can be no peace
Nor genuine love
While our minds are policed
Homes raided
Leaders jailed
And our sons and daughters murdered

O where are the minstrels now,
Those compliant clowns
Who jest while scavengers tear at our eyes
To trace the soul of our rebellion

Where am I
That I may shout defiance
Emerging from the hidden furnace of my spirit
Calling an aggrieved people towards rebirth
And insurrection
Against these nocturnal beasts
Who guard our dreams
And command our poems
To kneel before their guns

Deluge

My heart
Could have burst its banks
With a mad tide of longing,
Flooding streets, homes
Where people laughed,
Contented, undisturbed
So dark a tide
It would drown their dreams

How I hated distance, space
When every ticking hour
Was hollowed out
By hunger's keen blade
Jealousy,
Anger

I dared not meet lovers
Strolling in each other's shadows
Mine were furtive glances of envy
Rushing waves
Rising, falling
To rattle the roots
Of their bliss
How could they be happy
While I was sad

Softly

Cry softly my love
As we burn in the storm
Love is sweet,
Bitter
We are the debris,
The litter
The storm abates
Fire cleanses the soul
Wanderers in the wind
Tomorrow belongs to us

Morning

It is morning
The heavy veil of darkness
Lies tattered at my feet
Ghosts of unspoken emotion
And unsung songs
Hobble emaciated
Through the passage of my soul,
Crying to be touched, to be renewed
With the fervour of new life

I would have sung you a love song
But for fear you were hardened
By your understanding of love
And in my weakness
And in my grief
I remained silent
As you receded into the velvet night
God, how I rummaged the stars
In search of your eyes,
Praying for, yet dreading the morning light

Ah, but morning has come
And cinders of unrequited passion
Lie at the hearth of expediency,
The wounds of empty dreams
Are salted by tears of longing and need
When will love come again to rebuke
These uncaring, insensitive winds
That mock my vigil
At the altar of your heart

It is morning
And I miss you

Your gift

Your gift
    Warm,
    Alive against my flesh
    Weaves a virgin ecstasy
    Cleansing eyes
    Blinded by arrogance

In my hands
    Through my fingers
    I once let slip
    A vital dream
    And now
    A parchment inscribed with pain
    Lies crumpled
    At the horizon of my heart

But it was in your gift
    Prostrate
    Before the burning clouds,
    That I felt the fire rain down
    To singe your soul
    And mine

Kumbaya
A victory song

High,
The long-awaited uhuru eagle
Spreads its eager pinions
To herald the coming glory
Proudly
Serenely our fraternal flag
Flutters in the fresh winds
Singing our final Kumbaya
Across sleeping streams
Quenching ancient thirsts,
Feeding our hungry dreams

Kumbaya, my beautiful land
Kumbaya, my silent people
Kumbaya, my victory flag
Kumbaya Africa

Were this frightened pen a barrel
And these fiery phrases bullets,
You would have long buried my song
Beneath the sacred shadow
Of the beloved black-green-and-gold
Kumbaya,
The mighty eagle soars again
To stir the resting rivers
With bursts of victory songs
To purge our pain
And sweep the stubborn weed
Into the roaring seas

Elegy for Beirut

Where was I
On that grim night
When the gun-mongers
Danced in the blood
Of Palestinian exiles

Where was I
If only to fling
A handful of stones
At those killers

Blow loud the ramshorn
Snuff out the unholy candles
The dying
Is not over yet
Palestine shall be avenged!

Freedom Fighters

Unkindly bullets
Forge their passage
Through dark leaves
Hunting the soldiers
Martyred in the cause of liberty

You whose AKs are ballpens,
Write of their courage
And of the gift of their love
Laid on the altar of sacrifice
Cover them with tender words
To soothe the longing hearts
That pine for the native earth

Build them stout barricades
With your firm phrases,
Bathe their wounds in the healing flow of tears

And let the flag they died for
Flutter high above the unmarked graves
Carrying to posterity Africa's noblest
O my land
O my people in bondage
Behold
The Freedom Fighters ...

Sometimes

we need the spiritual retreat
to quell the seas of discontent
that rumble beneath our feet

Giovanni
On the birth of my son

Yesterday,
>You were but a thought in our minds
>A clot of life
>In your sweet mother's womb
>Touched by my spark
>Nourished by my flame

Today,
>A child in our arms
>Feeling the nipple
>Drinking the milk of our twilight
>Carrying the mark of our slavery

Tomorrow,
>A warrior
>Burning the bush with your blood
>Azanian son
>Carrying along a nation's song
>A singing tree
>Fighting tyranny
>For the right to be free

Our sons, our daughters

African rivers
    Stir a love song
    Deep in my bones

    Sacred land
    Broken beauty
    Plundered pride
    Seeking refuge in the drum

    Speaking of sacrifice
    And the unrepentant beast
    That must be silenced
    With the ritual blade of defiance

    We raise our plumes
    For our sons
    And our daughters

Zimbabwean Love Song

Sing and dance
Sons, daughters of Zimbabwe

It is the call of a timeless glory
And the beat of the native song
That beckoned you to struggle on

Nana Zimbabwe
It was your dance of daring feet
Which set the bush ablaze,
Made the dying sweet

Sing and dance
Daughters and sons of Zimbabwe
It is the rooster that sings of children
Marching against the wind

The white night is dead
Freedom walks in the sunrise
And in the glow of an eternal love song

Bitter seed

A bitter seed they sow
These pretorian creatures of darkness

Seed whose contagion
Blots the sky
With clouds of dread

Yet I can hear the whistle
In the wind
Singing across tyrant frontiers
Echoing our final call

There is no charity in chains
No comfort in bondage
The soul is obedient to fate
And gunpowder
Cannot tame the hearts that cry

It is time we were free

Salute the warrior
For our Freedom Fighters

The Spear is broken,
Dark streams pour out their contents
Across the barren sands
Where hope lies wounded
And love is a shattered song
Salute the warrior
Motionless on the battlefield
Shorn of life
Yet living evermore
He who gave his last
Gave his sacred best
That we might be free
Carrying our load
He wrote our destiny

Sleep well my flesh
Congeal the blood
And mark the spot
Where comrades fell
Where riveted hippos shot
Their dum-dum hell
Sleep well my country
It is not over yet
In the long black night
We nurse the agonising seed
And wait the unfailing dawn
To inflame the frightened breed
Who cringe to brutality
And to murder

The Spear is broken
And solemn graves

Heavy with the foetus of vengeance
Cry out against the uncaring foe:
It is not over yet
It is not over yet

Namibian Love Song
For SWAPO

Must we cry for you Namibia
When all around us
Maidens ululate your praise
From Libya to Dar es Salaam
From Angola to Maputo,
Zimbabwe to Azania

The stars dance for Nujoma
The moon sings for Ja-Toivo
A sacred love song!

    Lift up your dreams
    On the wings of desert winds
    Freedom is a cactus flower
    Nourished by the juice
    of Namibian lives
    Sprouting anew
    On dry riverbeds

        Undying now, the fighters
        Inflamed for the hour
        Marching ahead
        To meet the horizon
        Of Namibian glory
        There,
        Where the sun
        Never sets

A gift of words
For Judith

BELOVED,
    I'm told you no longer laugh
    That every stride, every step you take
    Is a journey into pain.

    I understand, it is the same with me.

    If you find some comfort
    From this gift of words,
    Void of poetic beauty as they are,
    Lacking form and rhythm
    But pouring from a heart
    Bursting with deep fervour,
    I will find some peace.

    Yesterday I saw women weep
    As we sang the anthem
    And I thought of you
    Crying that cold, lean night
    When the blue-coats took me away
    Because I refused to kneel.

    Do you remember?

    And in the grey courtroom
    You hid swollen eyes
    Behind dark glasses
    Forcing a smile
    To warm a million hearts.

    These lines then for you

Who stood in my shadow
During those cruel years
When I cried in my sleep
Gnashing teeth until I bled
Waking to see you sitting beside me.

And so,
    My beloved
    If you find a little comfort
    From this gift of words
    Look up, say yes
    And every feeble line will become immortal
    Like the truth men are dying for.

    Look up, say yes

I am nothing

I am nothing
I have nothing
Neither gold nor jewel to give you
Save these mad words
These erratic, impulsive stanzas
Men call poems
Trapped, bound
In the asylum of my heart
Stark,
Raving phrases
Tormented verbs
In search of logic
This breath is all I possess:
My beginning and my end.
Swaddled in song
I am nothing, my love
Yet just yesterday
You shared a dream.
Giving meaning to a life
Held down by pain

For you these lines
As gifts of deepest thanks
Take them,
Hold and pacify
The rumbling discontent
That shakes my frightened leaves

I offered so little
You gave so much
Now a million pianos sing
To appease the yearning furnace in my soul,

And quieten the querulous quill

I am nothing
>	I have nothing
>	But a love song
>	To touch your eyes
>	With passionate blood
>	Rushing through the vein of my pen,
>	Creating a life of words
>	Unending,
>	Infinite

>	I am something, now
>	I have you

Exiles
For Serote, Brutus & Makeba

Azanian exiles
weeping against the moon,
traversing the shores of strange lands
standing attention to foreign flags
alienated, tolerated nomads
sleeping in cars, park benches
or dining with kings,
I pine for you
with longing that eats my spirit,
tears out my eyes

Hearts reaching out
across the dark distances
where emotions are imprisoned
in the breast
voices crying where others are silent

I hunger for the fire-glow
of your comradeship, and
though our graves
have long been dug out
we smile at death

What some men call beauty
we call pain

Home is no longer home
but a cemetery
for unlived, unrealised dreams
where children seek shade
under trees of dead bones

By the river
by the sea
my soul awaits your home-coming

I am not estranged
from your anguish
you who weep
against the moon
and make your bed
on bramble bush,
I pine for you
with longing
that eats my eyes
and tears out my spirit

I will think of you

In these grievous times
When men in blue
rattle heavy keys at our doors
and take away our sons, our daughters,
pain is an eternity for the lost and the lonely.

I will think of you
when winter breaks the twigs
and dark leaves fall to enrich our cause
strengthen our roots.

I shall speak of you
standing in the twilight
shadowless,
my brother, my sister, blood of my blood
grasping those silent yesterdays
when in innocence
you made your bed on the wind
and talked with God.

I shall call your name
when a new bright sun
lights upon our darkness;
when broken chains glitter like polished gems
against the dark of our skins.

I will think of you
and sing of our days together
dying for a song
holding high our imperishable dreams
and your beauty
and your truth,
eternal like God.

A Song for Mandela

Inside of me
> in this blackened casket
> wounds lie sealed like bodies in a vault
> Shouts of anger crackle like flames
> in the fireplace of injustice

Beneath me
> impatient tremors burst out
> to break the dry olive branch of peace
> sold at the marketplace of deception

Around me
> the precious womb that bled me to life
> flesh that clothed my soul
> and gave it wings
> Yet even a mother's love
> is fragile to torment and to terror

Beside me
> heavy footfalls of running men
> cries of thwarted souls rush like restless rain
> from the skies of despair

Near me
> I hear the staunch march of anxious feet
> carrying the sounds of defiance
> Not alone, God, not alone
> will we rise up to repossess our land
> Truth is witness to our wrath
> and our commitment
> Evil has had its day

Beside me
      around and beneath me
      inside this burning self
      where impatient drums
      beat a martial song
      I hear Mandela singing:
      Unzima lomtwalo
      Ufuna amadoda namakhosikazi

We have been here before

When the first sun rose
It found us awake and waiting.
Long before others came to these hills
Our footsteps shaped the landscape
Tamed the buffalo and the gemsbok
We rode the wind
We silenced the hurricane
Look at us,
We have been here before.

We raised our temples
On the shifting sands of Mali
We traded in the busy, buzzing byways of Timbuktu
And on the cobbled lanes of Memphis
Our camels passed through the Needle's Eye.
We have been here before;
Our women bathed in milk and honey
Covered their bodies in gold and copper dust
And perfumes of myrrh and incense
Long before others came to our shores.

We hung on the Horn of Africa
Walked through the red sands of Somalia
And from the purple hills and valleys of Gondar
In ancient Ethiopia, our songs and supplications
Echoed across the perennial pyramids.

Ah, the pyramids,
Those timeless, glorious symbols
Of African civilisation.
These hands, our hands
Dark and lovely as the first night
Cut the stone that built the pyramids.
We have been here before.

Our warriors faced the scourge and might of the Scorpion
We thwarted his dominion over Africa
And reclaimed the ancient threads
Of our knowledge and gifts to humankind
Long before other conquerors came.

We removed the barriers of ignorance and isolation
'No people or nation are the sole architects
Of their own lives or their own destinies…'
We warned the seers, the high priests and the pharaohs
But they heeded not.

We washed our wounds in the Nile
We slept in the streets of Egypt
We slept under the wings of the Scarab
We made love to Nefertiti
Yes, look at us,
We have been here before.

Our eyes were stark, black stars
Raging in the night,
Tempests of rebellion
Ancient as life,
Long before the Serpent
Came to our children in the Garden
We looked at God
And saw our image in His eyes.

We have been here before.

***

www.ingramcontent.com/pod-product-compliance
Lightning Source LLC
Chambersburg PA
CBHW070734230426
43665CB00016B/2237